The Wright Brothers

by Anna Sproule

Picture Credits:
Austin Brown/Aviation Picture Library: 23, 47, 58 (below); The Bettmann Archive: 6-7, 33, 35, 44; The Bridgeman Art Library: 54-5; Mary Evans Picture Library: 4, 9, 12, 24, 50-1, 56-7; Exley Publications Photo Library: 16-7 (Nick Birch); Henry Ford Museum: 26, 39, 53; Library of Congress: 28, 34, 37, 40; NHPA: 30-1 (Manfred Daneggar), 43 (Stephen Dalton); Popperfoto: 31; Ann Ronan Picture Library: 11, 18-21; The Royal Aeronautical Society: 49; The Science Museum: 10; The Science Photo Library: 38 (Dale Boyer/Nasa), 39 (Dr Gary Settles), 58 (John Ross); The Smithsonian Institute: 48; Townley Hall Art Gallery and Museum: 13; Zeta: 59.

Acknowledgements

Extracts from *The Conquest of the Air* by C.L.M. Brown, OUP, 1927, reprinted with permission of Oxford University Press.

Extracts from *Interpretive History of Flight* by M.J.B. Davy, reprinted with permission of the Science Museum.

Extracts from *The Papers of Wilbur and Orville Wright*, ed. Marvin W. McFarland, McGraw-Hill, 1953.

Extracts from *The Wright Brothers: Heirs of Prometheus*, ed. R. Hallion, published by the National Aeronautical & Space Center (originally published in *Flying and the Aero Club of America Bulletin*, 1913).

Extracts from *Airborne at Kitty Hawk* by Michael Harrington, reprinted with permission of MacMillan Publishing Company (originally published by Cassell & Co. Ltd, London, 1953).

Extracts from *The Wright Brothers* by Fred C. Kelly, reprinted with permission of Harrap Publishing Group Ltd and Harcourt, Brace Jovanovich Inc.

Published in Great Britain in 1990
by Exley Publications Ltd,
16 Chalk Hill, Watford,
Herts WD1 4BN, United Kingdom.

Copyright © Exley Publications, 1990

British Library Cataloguing in Publication Data
Sproule, Anna.
The Wright brothers.
  1. Aviation. Wright, Orville, *1871-1948*
     & Wright, Wilbur *1867-1912*
  I. Title.   II. Series.
  629.130922

ISBN 1-85015-229-2

Series editor: Helen Exley.
Picture research: Elizabeth Loving.
Editing: Margaret Montgomery.
Typeset by Brush Off Studios,
St Albans, Herts AL3 4PH.
Printed and bound in Hungary.

The Wright Brothers

The story of the struggle to build and fly the first successful aeroplane

Anna Sproule

Le Petit Journal

Le Petit Journal
CHAQUE JOUR — 6 PAGES — 5 CENTIMES

Administration : 61, rue Lafayette

Les manuscrits ne sont pas rendus

5 CENTIMES SUPPLÉMENT ILLUSTRÉ **5** CENTIMES

Le Petit Journal agricole, 5 cent. ~~ La Mode du Petit Journal, 10 cent.
Le Petit Journal illustré de la Jeunesse, 10 cent.

On s'abonne sans frais dans tous les bureaux de poste

ABONNEMENTS

	SIX MOIS	UN AN
SEINE et SEINE-ET-OISE..	2 fr.	3 fr. 50
DÉPARTEMENTS..........	2 fr.	4 fr. »
ÉTRANGER.............	2 50	5 fr. »

Dix-neuvième Année   DIMANCHE 30 AOUT 1908   Numéro 928

L'AÉROPLANE DE WILBUR WRIGHT EN PLEIN VOL

The hungry wind

The wind was the enemy. Cold and hungry, it came roaring out of the north across the sand-flats, driving plumes of loose sand before it. From the doorway of their hut, the two brothers watched the sand blow.

In its shed close by, their flying machine waited, trembling in the wind that gusted through the timbers. It had already survived one crash. But that was in weather as calm and gentle as a summer's morning. Today was different. Today – the seventeenth of December, 1903 – the wind was roaring over the North Carolina coast at a speed approaching gale force.

Still watching the twirling sand-devils, one of the men suddenly spoke. "We won't have to climb the hill. We can launch it from here."

The other one nodded. It was true. To get up enough speed for that first launch, they'd started the machine on a sand dune. It had run downhill, taken off – and stalled. Today, though, the wind would do the work. It would fling the machine up like a kite: a stringless kite, thrust forward by an engine, ready to challenge gravity and fly where it wished.

The two men had designed the engine themselves. They had designed every part of the aircraft that waited for them in the shed – experimenting, researching, testing their findings. Now, just one great experiment remained.

The wind wasn't the only hungry one on that desolate coast. Wilbur and Orville Wright were hungry, too – for action. The wind would be their friend, not their enemy. It would speed their take-off, soften their landing.

The two brothers grinned at each other. They'd waited around long enough. It was time to go.

Opposite: The aircraft in the picture was demonstrated in France in 1908. Its pilot was an American named Wilbur Wright who, with his brother, had built the first successful full-sized aeroplane of all time, five years earlier. They would revolutionize science, so the French press said. In fact, they would revolutionize the world.

The brothers who conquered the air: Wilbur and (opposite) Orville Wright, of Dayton, Ohio. Wilbur was the older one by four years. Silent and highly-strung, he was a self-taught scientist of genius. Orville was more outgoing, and had a natural talent for business. It was this mixture of gifts, brought together in a lifelong partnership, that gave the world its first aeroplane.

Orville's turn

Their decision made, the Wrights bustled their little camp into life. They checked the wind again. They hung up a signal to call the life-saving men from their base a mile away across the sand. The life-guards had been in on the plan from the start; they couldn't be left out now.

Next came the machine itself. Its builders hauled it out of the shed and checked it over. The wings, the struts, the wires that linked the controls: they were all as they should be. The propellers moved easily. So did the lever that controlled the front rudder, sticking out in front of the wings. The sledge-like runners on which the machine stood showed no signs of their accident a few days earlier. The machine would do.

The Wrights arranged it astride its launching rail, and anchored it with a length of wire. To keep it steady, Wilbur shoved a prop under its right-hand wing. A few feet away, Orville set up his camera. As he settled the tripod's legs firmly into the sand, the life-guards hurried into the camp, laughing and shouting.

They watched intently as the two brothers started the machine's engine. It ran with a steady, reassuring throb, warming up for the moment when it would take the machine down the rail and into the air. And the Wrights looked at each other.

"Go on, Orville," Wilbur said. "I've had my turn. It's yours now."

Time to go

Cautiously, Orville eased himself into the machine, and stretched out flat on the lower wing. The wind, gusting straight into his eyes, scattered sand on his eyelashes. So he looked downward, at the tiny pebbles on the ground below his face.

In a last check of the controls, he moved his hips gently from side to side. Yes: the cradle in which he lay shifted with him, twisting and dipping the wing surfaces at his sides. At the end of the right-hand one stood Wilbur, waiting to steady it as the machine moved down the rail.

It really was time to go now. Orville reached out and released the machine's wire anchor.

In free flight

He was moving. He was moving forward at walking pace. No, faster than that. From the corner of his eye, Orville could see his brother loping alongside. Loping faster. Beginning to run.... And, suddenly, Wilbur wasn't there any more.

The machine was airborne.

It was going too high! Quickly, Orville moved the lever that led to the front rudder. Instantly, there was the ground, only ten feet below him and rising fast. Desperately, Orville dragged the lever back.

It was like being hit in the stomach. With a sickening jolt, the aircraft halted its crazy plunge. The earth fell away, the world filled with sky as the machine surged upward again. A gust caught its wings with a smack, and it surged higher.

Orville gave another touch to the lever. With dizzy speed, the machine tilted in the air. Then it swooped for the ground like a demented swallow. Another correction, and it tilted up again. And down. And up....

And down. With a crunch, a final crashing jolt, and a great spray of sand, the machine slammed itself on to the earth. And stayed there. Dazed and breathless, Orville crawled out and looked back along the way he'd come.

The conquest of the air

He had only flown a hundred-and-twenty feet. He had only been airborne for twelve seconds. But that short distance and that tiny timespan added up to nothing less than victory.

Orville and his brother had gone where no one had ever gone before. They had built a heavier-than-air machine that could carry a person in free flight. It kept itself in the air by its own power, and its movements could be controlled – roughly, but still decisively – by its pilot. Between them, they had

"To Wilbur and Orville Wright – whose courage and genius made it possible – was left the final glory of producing the first successful flying machine. They succeeded, by their own exertions, in doing what others were mainly thinking and talking about."

M.J.B. Davy, from "Interpretive History of Flight"

Opposite, top left: In a test on the effect of flight on living creatures, a hot-air balloon designed by the Montgolfier brothers of France makes a trial flight over Versailles in the 1780s. The basket contained a sheep, a rooster and a duck. The sheep trod on the rooster during the flight, but all three "passengers" returned to earth unharmed.

designed and created the world's first successful full-sized aeroplane.

On the sands south of Kitty Hawk, North Carolina, Wilbur and Orville Wright had conquered the air.

"First in the history of the world"

Looking back at that December day almost ninety years ago, it's easy to see why the Wrights' achievement was so momentous. Saying why it was so momentous is, oddly enough, much harder.

Orville's own report, published in 1913, still remains the best way of defining what the brothers had actually achieved. "This flight," he wrote, "only lasted twelve seconds, but it was nevertheless the first in the history of the world in which a machine carrying a man had raised itself by its own power into the air in full flight, had sailed forward without reduction of speed, and had finally landed at a point as high as that from which it started."

Every word in this complicated sentence is important – and what Orville doesn't say is as important as what he does. For instance, he doesn't say he was the first man to fly. That record had been taken over a hundred years earlier by two Frenchmen, Pilâtre de Rozier and the Marquis of Arlandes.

Nor does Orville claim to have designed the first machine to leave the ground successfully. It was another pair of brothers who had done that. Also French, they were two paper manufacturers named Joseph and Étienne Montgolfier. In the early 1780s, the Montgolfiers had started experimenting with the properties of hot air. By June 1783, they were ready to demonstrate the results of their work to their home town of Annonay.

Before the townspeople's flabbergasted eyes, they filled a large balloon of cloth and paper with hot air from a fire, and released it. The balloon soared skywards, and rose to the tremendous height of six thousand feet. When the air inside it cooled, it returned to earth over a mile away – and was ripped up by terrified peasants, who thought it was the Devil. A few months later, in November,

Top right, and bottom: In the nineteenth century, daring spirits took their balloons further and higher. The balloonists in the upper picture reached a height of 14,000 feet.

Flying fever in Britain: the first Aeronautical Society show in 1868. Of the many designs developed by hopeful inventors, only the fixed-wing aircraft on the left would have any real future in flight. Although birds can power themselves through the air with flapping wings, a human's muscles are not strong enough.

de Rozier and the Marquis had wafted over Paris in a "Montgolfière" to become the world's first aviators.

With their pioneering flight, the human race realized an ambition it had held for centuries.

Heavier than air

Ballooning quickly caught on, both for sport and warfare. But, even as they moved through the air, the pioneers knew they were still at the air's mercy.

A lighter-than-air machine – a balloon – could only go where the wind blew it.

Some inventors tried to control their huge craft with inefficient, steam-powered propellers. But other people had started to wonder if controlled flight could be achieved in machines that were *heavier* than air, rather than lighter. All through the 1800s, flying enthusiasts worked at this revolutionary idea and, one by one, inched the frontiers of possibility back.

They built model gliders that, equipped with wings, glided through the air like birds. They built gliders big enough to carry people – and kill them. They also produced model aircraft, powered by steam. One experimented with another source of power, the newly-developed petrol engine. And, all the time, they worried away at the baffling, tantalizing principles that underlay the science of mechanical flight.

By the end of 1903, these scientists, engineers and intrepid bird-men had come within inches of the final prize: powered flight, controlled by a human operator. But it was Wilbur and Orville Wright, two bicycle-makers from the American Midwest, who reached out and took it. And, in doing so, they changed the world for ever.

Everything in people's lives – from eating to war – has always been affected by the speed at which they and their goods can travel. What Wilbur and Orville started at Kitty Hawk would end with people being able to travel faster than sound. The Wrights speeded the world up out of all recognition.

The electric anti-gravity device: another design that never worked! The wheel turned by the aviator in this picture generated static electricity that – in theory – lifted the machine into the air.

The house on Hawthorn Street

Wilbur Wright was born on April 16, 1867, on a farm in Indiana, USA. Orville came into the world on August 19, 1871, in a white frame house in Dayton, Ohio. They were the third and fourth sons of a clergyman, Milton Wright, who was soon to become a bishop. After some shuttling between Ohio, Indiana and Iowa, the bishop settled down with his wife and children in the Dayton house, and made it the family home.

With its shutters and painted clapboard walls, the house on leafy Hawthorn Street looked just like the others in the area. And Wilbur and Orville's childhood seemed every bit as ordinary. They went to school, and sometimes played truant. They did household chores to earn some money, and spent what they earned on their hobbies. Wilbur's passion was skating. Orville, a born entrepreneur, went in for schemes like collecting scrap metal.

They also made things. With his friends, Orville did a brisk trade in home-made kites. Wilbur, meanwhile, invented a machine for folding newspapers. He made a little money by folding the pages of a local church magazine: eight pages an issue, to be folded and trimmed every week. It was desperately boring, and Wilbur had better things to do. So he automated the process, powering his invention with a treadle of the sort then used for sewing-machines.

The Chinese top

In fact, making things was in the family. The boys' mother, Susan, could make and mend anything, including a sledge she built for her sons. Her husband, the bishop, did not share her practical gifts. But he applauded them in his sons – and encouraged others. He delighted in his children's inquiring minds. Wilbur and Orville, pursuing one hobby after another, could pillage his library for any book they wanted.

The bishop sparked off one of their projects himself. In the late 1870s, he came home one day with a present he'd bought for them. He tossed the little object into the air – and, as Wilbur and Orville stared open-mouthed, it soared up to the ceiling.

Today, the bishop's present would be called a model helicopter. It was then known as a "Chinese flying top": a propeller on a spindle, powered by pulling on a tightly-wound string. No one knew when Chinese tops had first come west from Asia. But children in Europe had been playing with them since the early 1400s. The Wrights' toy was the very latest model, powered by a twisted rubber band.

The boys played with their fragile top until it

Flying tops designed as tiny model helicopters were delighting children five hundred years before the first full-scale helicopter ever flew.

Opposite: Another children's toy that mastered the air long before the invention of powered flight.

broke. Then, fired with enthusiasm, they made copy after copy. They called them "bats". The bat craze passed in the end; Wilbur, getting ambitious, made them bigger and bigger, then found they didn't fly. But the memory of the tiny original and its soaring flight never quite faded. Nor did the fascination it aroused.

The four-year gap

Years later, Wilbur would say that Orville and he worked, played and thought together from childhood. Orville, the more out-going of the two, remembered things differently. Early on, he recalled, they found the four years between them an awkward gap to bridge. Projects like the "bats" had sometimes spanned it. But, most of the time, Wilbur had stayed on his side of the divide, immersed in his sport and his books.

School interested him more than it did his brother; both of them were bright, but Wilbur enjoyed school work enough to volunteer for extra study in Greek and mathematics. Orville, just as gifted but more rebellious, got into trouble so thoroughly that one school actually threw him out.

By this time, kites had long been replaced by home printing. With a friend, Orville set up a kitchen-table printing firm, building his own press and producing handbills for Dayton shopkeepers. The venture was so successful that, very soon, he gave himself over to printing heart and soul. Two summers came and went; attached to a local printer, Orville worked ten hours a day during his time off school.

For a long while, it must have looked as if the intellectual Wilbur would go one way while Orville, the businessman in the making, would go another. But then something happened that changed their lives for ever.

The partnership

Its cause was Wilbur's love of skating: both the style and skill of figure-skating, and the speed of ice-hockey. But all skating came to an end when, during an ice-hockey match, a team-member's stick smashed him full in the face. The accident cost him all the front teeth in his upper jaw. His face mended – but then it was discovered that he had heart trouble as well. Wilbur said goodbye to the skating rink and the gym, and settled as best he could into the life of a semi-invalid.

Susan Wright – once so resourceful and active – was by then also ill. Indeed, she was dying. Immobilized by his own heart trouble, Wilbur spent hours with his mother and looked after her devotedly. He also offered to help Orville design a new printing press. Weird though his design was, it still drew compliments from a professional printer who inspected it. "It works all right," the printer said. "But I still don't understand *why* it works."

Susan Wright died in 1889. The house in Hawthorn Street felt strangely empty now, for the two older boys had also left home. But, slowly, life began to feel more normal. Susan's place in the household was taken by the boys' sister, Katharine. The youngest of them all, she mothered and organized her father, Orville, and the slowly-recovering Wilbur.

Meanwhile, her two brothers were finding that the gap between them had somehow filled itself in. They liked the same things, they thought the same way. Even in the fiercest of arguments, they talked the same language. They were founding a partnership of mind and spirit that would last a lifetime.

The Wright Cycle Company

By this time, Orville was printing and publishing a local weekly newspaper. When he left school in 1890, he decided to earn his living from it. Wilbur joined him. But, two years later, they discovered an interest that was more absorbing: bicycling. The craze for cycling was then sweeping Europe and North America. Young people, especially, loved the freedom and independence it gave them, and Wilbur and Orville were no exceptions. Enthralled by their new hobby, they decided to

"Early in life the boys showed a mechanical turn of mind and, what was even more important, developed that scientific outlook necessary for pioneers in such a field. They were patient, careful and painstaking, and never took a step without first making sure that it was theoretically justified. This care was to be of the utmost value when they came to construct their machine."

John Canning, from "100 Great Lives".

The setting in which the world's first aeroplane was brought into existence: the Wright bicycle shop in Dayton, Ohio. The shop and its contents – like the highly-polished desk (right) that Wilbur and Orville used – are now on show at the Henry Ford Museum, Dearborn, Michigan.

change businesses. They would sell bicycles.

In 1892, they set themselves up as the Wright Cycle Company. At first, they just traded in cycles; then, as the business prospered, they started making and repairing them. And, in 1897, Orville began to hatch even grander schemes. In Europe, the engineers Karl Benz and Gottfried Daimler were producing carriages powered, not by horses, but by the newly-invented petrol engine. This, Orville thought, might be even more profitable than making cycles. But Wilbur talked him out of it.

It was just as well – for, by now, a fresh hobby had started claiming the brothers' energy. In 1896, they'd heard about another German engineer with a new line in transport. His name was Otto Lilienthal, and he was trying to fly. What's more, he was succeeding.

Sir George Cayley

People had, of course, been going up in balloons for over a century. But Lilienthal was experimenting with something else: with flight in a machine that was heavier than air. Nor was he the first.

Here, too, the story went back for years. It started soon after the first balloon flights, when an English baronet, Sir George Cayley, began a series of experiments. His first one focussed on the Chinese top – the same toy that would one day fascinate the Wright boys. In 1796, he built an improved version that could rise as high as ninety feet in the air. Then he went further. He started asking himself *how* things flew. Just what was it they did? What was flight really all about?

He studied birds' flight. Then, in 1804, he designed a model glider – based on a "common paper kite" – that would skim for sixty feet or so through the air. Next came a full-sized one that he successfully launched, unmanned, from a hill. Very much later, he would build an improved model and (so locals whispered darkly) order his terrified coachman to go up in it. The coachman survived, but gave in his notice the second he returned to earth!

"A bird is an instrument working in accordance with mathematical law, which instrument it is within the capacity of man to reproduce."
Leonardo da Vinci.

"It is very beautiful to see this noble white bird sail majestically from the top of a hill to any given point of the plane [sic] below it, according to the set of its rudder, merely by its own weight, descending in an angle of about eighteen degrees with the horizon."
Sir George Cayley, describing his full-size glider in flight.

In this cartoon of 1883, a French artist imagined how people would travel in the 1950s. Although his "air-cars" still looked like lighter-than-air machines, they were powered by the ultra-new petrol engine – just as the Wrights' machine would be.

Power, weight and air

In 1809, Cayley started publishing his findings. In an essay called *On aerial navigation*, he defined heavier-than-air flight in a sentence that became famous. The whole problem, he wrote, came down to this: making a surface "support a given weight by the application of power to the resistance of the air."

18

To explain what he meant, he used the example of a bird's wings, stretched out for soaring into the wind. As the bird flew forward, its wings met the wind at a slight angle. And the wind, which was moving horizontally, acted on this angled surface to lift the bird up. In other words, it supported the bird's weight – and the bird soared high in the sky.

Cayley's interest in heavier-than-air flight later spread to a textile engineer named William Henson. In 1842, Henson summed up the baronet's thinking much more clearly than Cayley had himself. "If," he wrote, "any light and flat, or nearly flat, article be projected or thrown edgeways in a slightly inclined position, the same will rise on the air till the force exerted is expended." And it would go on rising – as long as two conditions were met. Its front edge had to go on being higher than the back one, and the power that moved it forward had to be maintained.

A flight that never took place. This steam-powered flying machine was invented in the 1840s by William Henson. To drum up publicity (and money) for his project, he had pictures printed that showed the aircraft steaming over London. But, when tried out, the test model failed to fly.

Two more designs for conquering the air in birdman style, with flapping wings. The one above uses a form of pedal power. The machine on the opposite page was tested by its inventor in London. When launched from a height, it instantly crashed to the ground, killing its inventor.

Henson was talking here about throwing something. But, as he knew, there were other forms of power than that exerted by the flick of a wrist. One sort lay in a bird's muscles, while the factories of the Industrial Revolution were driven by another – steam.

Henson reasoned that what muscle-power did for birds, steam could do for humans. And, in the 1840s, he produced a design for a bird-shaped "Aerial Steam Carriage". It was a breakthrough in more ways than one for, at a time when flying machines took the shape of huge, bulging balloons, the Steam Carriage had wings.

When it was tested, Henson's design did not work. Discouraged, he gave up his experiments and emigrated to the United States. But his partner, John Stringfellow, carried on with the work and, in 1848, came up with a new experimental model. Ten feet across from wing-tip to wing-tip, and also powered by steam, it was designed to be launched along a tight-stretched cable.

When tested in an old lace-factory, Stringfellow's machine shot along the wire, reached the end …

and continued upward under its own power until it flew into the canvas placed to catch it. It was the first powered model aircraft in history to achieve free flight.

Lilienthal's obsession

Cayley, Henson and Stringfellow were not the only people to investigate the riddle of flight in the nineteenth century. Many others followed them, ranging from distinguished scientists to out-and-out crackpots. And, in the 1860s, a boy named Otto Lilienthal joined the list. With his brother, he tried making slip-on wings out of wood. The wings were failures, but the boy went on working at the problem. When he grew up, it became an obsession.

By now a design engineer, he quickly realized that all the other inventors had something in common. They knew – or thought they knew – a lot about flight. But they knew almost nothing about *flying*. Flying was a practical activity. The way to learn practical activities is to do them. And the way to solve the puzzles set by the air was to get airborne.

The hump-backed curve

Like Cayley before him, Lilienthal started by studying birds. In 1889, he published his findings, in a work now thought of as the oldest textbook on mechanical flight. One of the most important things he found out concerned the shape of a flying wing: not its lengthwise shape, but the shape of its cross-section. A section through a bird's outstretched wing is not flat. Instead, it is "cambered": it rises in a shallow, humped curve, steeper on one side than on the other. This shape is called an aerofoil, and it is on the aerofoil that mechanical flight is based.

What actually happens when an aerofoil – an aircraft's wing – moves through the air? The air through which it's passing flows both above and below it. Because the aerofoil's top surface is bigger than its bottom one, the air there has further to flow. This means it flows faster.

"An object offers as much resistance to the air as the air does to the object."
Leonardo da Vinci.

Although they look so different, the wings of the owl on the left and the aircraft on the right have a lot in common. Look carefully at the middle picture of the owl. Can you see the slight upward slant its wings and body make towards the direction it's going? If you look at the aircraft, you can see the same thing. Both types of wing are also aerofoils, with a sharp camber on their upper side. The "flaps" curving down from the back of the aircraft's wings helped slow it down for landing; the extra flap jutting out from the wing's front edge helped keep it flying at this slower speed.

A law of physics, that's called Bernoulli's Principle, now comes into play. This law says that, when a moving gas or liquid is speeded up, the pressure it exerts on surfaces around it grows less. So the air moving over an aircraft wing exerts less pressure on it than the air moving underneath it.

The lowered pressure creates a suction effect above the wing, called "lift". As a result, the air moving over the aerofoil works from above to suck – or pull – the aerofoil up. Lift is a force that increases as an aerofoil's forward movement gets faster. So, the faster the aircraft flies, the stronger the upward pull on its wings becomes. Meanwhile, the air underneath the aerofoil is also pushing it up from below.

Lift and drag

But lift is not the only force operating on an aircraft in flight. It is all the time countered by gravity,

trying to pull the aircraft down to the ground. Another force – which counters the aircraft's forward thrust – is called "drag".

Drag is the name given to the friction applied by the air through which the aerofoil moves. Like lift, it increases with the wing's speed. So, while the air works to pull an aircraft up, it also works to pull it back.

This is where a wing's angle to the air – its "angle of attack", a slight upward slope – becomes so important. The best possible angle is the one that gives the aerofoil the biggest amount of lift and the least amount of drag. This angle changes all the time, depending on the speed at which the aerofoil is moving. If the angle becomes too flat, the lift starts to decrease, and the drag to grow. If the angle becomes much too sharp, things quickly get dangerous: the lift decreases, the drag becomes huge, and the aircraft stops flying. It stalls and, as flyers say, "falls out of the air".

"During take-off and landing, the wing shape needs to be very different to that needed for cruising. By adjusting the area of the flaps presented to the air, and their angle to it, a pilot is able to vary the amount of lift and drag generated by the wing to suit different phases of the flight."

David Macaulay and
Neil Ardley, from
"The Way Things Work", 1988.

The man who inspired the Wrights: Otto Lilienthal in flight, using his "double decker", or biplane, glider. The Wrights would adopt the biplane design for their own experiments in flight.

Lilienthal airborne

In 1891, after years of workbench experiments, Otto Lilienthal began to test the effects of lift and drag on himself. So he built an experimental aircraft: a glider of willow canes covered with cotton sheeting. Under the wings, it was equipped with padded "sleeves" through which Lilienthal thrust his arms.

With his cotton wings spread out around him, he climbed onto a springboard, jumped off – and found himself gliding through the air. Before long, he could fly a hundred yards, then more. He discarded the springboard and, instead, used steep hills for his take-offs. Then, in Berlin, he had an artificial hill built for him, fifty feet high, and used that.

He made flight after flight: the total reached the hundreds, then the thousands. And, with each one, his experience at handling the air grew. Lift and drag, he discovered, were not the whole story. He had to keep steady in the air as well. He found he could keep his glider balanced if he carefully moved his dangling body around.

By 1896, when his fame reached the United States (and the Wrights), he was planning a major ·improvement to his glider. He was going to power it with an engine. But, before he could install it, the danger he'd courted so long caught up with him.

In August, the great Lilienthal made a single mistake in the air. He tried to correct himself, failed and – from the height of fifty feet – plunged to his death.

"Otto Lilienthal was the first man to practise gliding persistently and scientifically, as a means whereby the aeroplane might be perfected, and controlled mechanical flight actually achieved.... Without his work, and especially without his example, it is doubtful whether the Wrights would have succeeded."

C.L.M. Brown, from "The Conquest of the Air".

"Sacrifices will have to be made."

The dying words of Otto Lilienthal; quoted in the "Wright Papers".

Spellbound

Far away in Dayton, the news of Lilienthal's death, and his obsession with flight, triggered something off in the Wright brothers. They had been mildly interested before; now, suddenly, they were spellbound by this magical idea of flight. They wanted to know more about it. They wanted to try it for themselves.

Brimming with questions, they went to start their researches at Dayton Public Library. They found little to help them. Doggedly, they kept on hunting and, in 1899, Wilbur finally wrote for help to the famous Smithsonian Institution in Washington.

The Smithsonian sent him back a reading list that covered much of what had been written on mechanical flight. Its starting-point was Leonardo da Vinci. And it ended with the very latest books on the subject: one by a French-born engineer and gliding enthusiast, Octave Chanute, and another by an American, Professor Samuel P. Langley. Langley had been working on mechanical flight for years. In 1896, he had even made a steam-powered model aircraft that had flown across three-quarters of a mile over Washington's Potomac River.

Now, at last, the Wright brothers had something to go on. It was summer, and the spring-time rush of the bicycle business was easing. So, like students before an exam, they pored over their books, cramming themselves with facts. But were they really facts? And why were there gaps in them? Fired with enthusiasm, Wilbur and Orville began to think things out for themselves.

The question of balance

Obviously, the question of balance was crucial. An aircraft that kept tipping from side to side in the air was worse than useless: it was dangerous. Lilienthal had died because he couldn't balance his flying machine. The brothers gnawed hungrily on the problem. And, very soon, they came up with a solution: a completely new one, untried by anyone else.

At work in the Dayton bicycle shop. In addition to their other gifts, Wilbur and Orville were outstanding technicians. If they had not been able to build the working parts for their great project, it would probably never have flown. Some of the problems they faced were awesomely difficult. They solved others very simply: once, they stuck some loose parts together with the glue used for bicycle repairs!

The answer was to change the shape of the machine's wings during flight.

If, the Wrights reasoned, a flying machine tipped over to the left, its left-hand wing would be lower than the right-hand one. But, if the shapes of the wings could be changed, the left-hand wing could be altered so that it met the air at a sharper angle than its right-hand twin. A sharper angle meant greater lift: the left-hand wing would rise, the right-hand one would sink, and the machine would again be flying in a balanced way.

So far, so good; but how could this shape-changing business be done? It was while they were wondering about it that Wilbur was hit by inspiration.

A box for an inner tube

At the shop, the peak trading months were almost over. But punctures are never out of season! One day, a customer came in to buy a new inner tube for his bicycle. Wilbur fetched one, packed in its narrow cardboard box, and took it out. Then, idly turning the box between his fingers, he stood chatting to the purchaser.

Suddenly, he looked at what his hands were doing. They were holding the box at either end, by the corners. And as the chat drifted on, he was twisting the two ends in different directions. One moment, he could see the top left-hand end of the box, and the bottom right-hand one. A twist in the opposite direction, and the top right-hand end came into view.

It dipped down at the back, and up at the front. *Up at the front.*

Now, supposing the box were the right-hand and left-hand wings of an aircraft....

Wing-warping

The day of the inner-tube box marks the true start of the Wright brothers' great challenge to the air. Like Lilienthal, they knew that the only way to learn about flying was to fly. They now could fly more safely than Lilienthal had.

"By comparison with many more or less contemporary inventions, such as the telephone, the cinematograph and the transmission and reception of sound waves, which resulted from much patient research and skill in probing into the secrets of natural laws, the flying machine represents, in one sense, the greatest of all; for to solve the problem of mechanical flight it was necessary not so much to observe, as to learn how to defy the immutable law of gravity and actually to fly in the face of Nature."

M.J.B. Davy.

Wilbur's inspiration decided the pattern their work would now follow. During July and August 1899, they built a "double-decker" kite that imitated the box's shape. It measured five feet across, and was equipped with cords leading to its corners. Depending on how the cords were pulled, the kite's double wings twisted down at one end or another – just like the box had done.

In August, watched by a group of small boys, Wilbur tried it out on a patch of wasteland outside Dayton. He returned home well-satisfied: the idea, that the Wrights called "wing-warping", worked.

Within a few years, it would form the basis of the patent they'd file for their complete system of aircraft control. With the flexible wings replaced by a system of movable flaps, it is still used by aircraft today.

Enlisting an expert

From the very start, the brothers' aim had been clear. They'd enjoyed sports like skating and cycling; now they wanted to enjoy flying. Lilienthal, for all

The perfect place for flight trials: the sands of Kitty Hawk, North Carolina. Here, Orville (with his back to the camera) and Wilbur are flying their home-made glider as a kite. The small extra "wing" above their heads is the glider's rudder. Attached to the <u>front</u> of the aircraft, it gave the glider fore-and-aft balance.

his experience, had only put in five hours of actual practice in the air. The Wrights planned to have many, many more – and the way ahead was now open. They would build a bigger, stronger kite: a kite big enough and strong enough to carry a human passenger. In other words, a glider.

But kites need wind. A kite carrying a person needs plenty of wind, strong and steady; a sudden lull would be disastrous! The brothers worked out they needed a wind of 15 mph for their experiments. But where were they to find a flat, lonely place where winds of this speed were common? The Wrights first asked Washington's Weather Bureau for information and, in reply, received a list of places and wind speeds. Then Wilbur had an even better idea. He wrote to Octave Chanute – and, without knowing it, enlisted their most important ally in their battle against the air.

The perfect place

In Chicago, Chanute was delighted to hear from a fellow-enthusiast. He wrote back warmly to his unknown correspondent in Dayton, with helpful suggestions. Sand-hills, he said, were an ideal practice ground, while sea-breezes were reliably steady. How about the coast of California – or, even better, South Carolina?

By this time, it was spring again: the spring of 1900. As spring turned into summer, the brothers moved from thinking into action. They began to build their glider; they got out their wind-speed tables again and looked through them. Coasts, sand-hills, and somewhere not too far from Ohio.... And one place struck them at once.

Chanute had been almost right. It was on the coast of North Carolina, rather than South, on one of the long, sandy islands that separated the coastal lagoons from the Atlantic Ocean. It had a weather bureau and two life-saving stations; it also had a post office and about twenty houses, dotted here and there among the dunes. Apart from the sand, the wind, and the sea, it had little else.

Its name was Kitty Hawk – and it was perfect.

"The attitude adopted by the Wright brothers was that every theory previously advanced must be tested and proved by practical experiment, and the courage and thoroughness of their work has been described as a perfect example of the way in which research should be conducted."

M.J.B. Davy.

Science copying nature: the slightly curved underside of the glider's wings (right) closely imitates that of the swan's. The Kitty Hawk photograph shows the launching procedure for gliding. The aviator here is Orville, with Wilbur (left) and a Kitty Hawk man for assistance.

By the start of September the brothers had everything ready. Orville, as they'd agreed, stayed on in Dayton to mind the shop, while Wilbur set up things on the coast. A few weeks later, it was Orville's turn to leave for North Carolina, taking with him a good supply of groceries. "They can't buy even tea or coffee or sugar at Kitty Hawk," Katharine Wright wrote to their father.

"I never did hear," she added later, "of such an out-of-the-way place."

The sands of Kitty Hawk

There was a sound like a thunderclap, and Orville woke with a start. The wind was getting up. The sides of the tent were flapping and banging around

"*At one and the same time they [the Wright brothers] were cautious plodding workers, romantic visionaries, and cool headed courageous adventurers. No one could have been better equipped by nature for the task which they so determinedly set themselves to accomplish.*"
C.L.M. Brown, from "The Conquest of the Air".

like laundry on a line. Above the flapping came a sizzling noise: outside, the sand would be blowing past again, turning the land into more of a desert every day. And, high above it all, came the dauntless singing of a mocking-bird.

Orville smiled to himself. He liked the mocking-bird. It lived in the low, wind-combed tree to which they'd fixed their tent. Nothing – not even the worst north-easter – could shift it. It was always there, singing.

On the camp-bed opposite, Wilbur was still asleep. His brother unrolled himself from his blankets, and checked the stove. Yes; still burning. The next thing was water for coffee. Orville – camp cook since he'd arrived – undid the tent flaps and peered outside.

Before him lay the reason why they'd come here in the first place: the restless, shifting sands of Kitty Hawk.

Orville rubbed his eyes and looked again. Where was the glider? They'd left it only a short distance away. But it was not there now. There was nothing to be seen but sand, mounded up in a smooth, unbroken hump. Exclaiming angrily, Orville came out of the tent at a crouching run.

The soaring machine

He found the machine almost at once. On his knees at the edge of the mound, probing and scrabbling frantically, he barked his fingers against something hard: something like a stick. It was only eight inches down. But who knew what damage that could do: a heavy layer of sand, eight inches deep, spread over ... what? Eighty square feet of cotton fabric? A hundred?

Doing sums in his head, Orville dug on furiously. Beside him, a grim-faced Wilbur appeared, and began to dig too.

Slowly, the object they called a "soaring machine" emerged. First came the wooden supports for the elevator, the front rudder they'd built on to give the glider fore-and-aft balance. Working back, they came to the upper wing: seventeen

feet wide, five feet deep, humped in a shallow, subtle curve from front to back, and covered with cotton sateen stretched over ash-wood ribs. Somewhere down below, past a cat's-cradle of steel wires, was the lower one – also curved and tightly stretched, but with a hole cut out of the middle, facing the rudder.

As the morning wore by, the brothers uncovered the top wing, dug down past the wooden uprights, dusted off the pale sateen, and slid the glider free. Anxiously, they checked it over for damage. But, miraculously, there was none: no tears, no breaks. The wind – still rushing by at 25 mph – was too good to miss. Lugging their machine between them, the brothers set out on their regular route south, to the sand dunes.

Dangerous? Wilbur – here seen in mid-glide – swore that it wasn't. But he hadn't always been so confident. The first time that the 1900 glider soared skywards with him, he panicked and yelled to Orville to get him down. He later laughed over the memory, but Lilienthal's death can never have been far from his mind.

The glider comes alive

The wind always seemed to be blowing at Kitty Hawk. The week the brothers first tested their glider, it had been blowing off and on at gale force. Sensibly, they dropped their plan to go up in their machine. Instead, they weighted it with chain and flew it on ropes, like a vast kite. They controlled the rudder with cords, pulling this way and that to make the glider dip or rise.

Quickly, their creation took on the power and personality of a live thing. Sometimes it behaved beautifully, soaring and dipping to order. Sometimes it went mad, plummeting earthwards with demonic frenzy. But, by the end of their stay on the sands, Wilbur and Orville felt they'd got its measure. They were ready to try flying in it.

The brothers now needed an assistant, and they found one in the shape of the Kitty Hawk postmaster, Bill Tate. The Tate family had been their friends from the first, feeding and housing them till they set up camp. The glider's sateen wings had even been finished on Mrs. Tate's sewing-machine.

The kitchen in the Wrights' camp building at Kitty Hawk. Here, Orville – who did all the camp cooking – was boss. Getting new supplies of food was always difficult, and there was never any fresh bread. So Orville taught himself to make scones, using the flour and baking pans shown in the picture.

For the manned gliding sessions, the Wrights and their helper went to the largest sand dunes on the island, four miles away. Called the Kill Devil Hills, they rose to a hundred feet above the surrounding flats: a perfect launching-point for a glider.

For each launch, they'd place the machine high up on the biggest dune, facing downhill. One of the brothers would climb onto the machine's lower wing, and lie flat in the middle. Tate and the other brother would position themselves at either end of the wings, lift the machine between them, and start running.

As the air started moving over and past the wings, the glider became airborne. The helpers let go, and the machine sailed majestically downhill, to land gently on the sand at the bottom.

Not as much as a bruise

It looked dangerous; in fact, Wilbur assured Chanute after, it was completely safe. Even though the machine sometimes flew at 30 mph, neither

The birthplace of modern aeroplane design – with a Dayton undertaker next door. Until the Wrights' invention became big business, everything the brothers did was on a modest scale. Their first glider was made for half the price of a man's suit. The cost of developing and making the aeroplane itself worked out at about the same price as buying an early motor-car: a big sum but not an enormous one. And their all-important research was fitted into gaps between the bicycling seasons.

he nor Orville got as much as a bruise. True, there were still a lot of things that puzzled them; Lilienthal's figures on lift, for instance, didn't seem to apply. But, after all, they had only done two minutes actual manned gliding; they would come back next year, and find out more.

In good spirits, Wilbur and Orville set out for home, leaving their machine behind. It was now Bill Tate's, to do with as he liked. Very soon, his two little girls appeared in brand-new frocks of best French sateen. Mrs. Tate's sewing-machine had been active again.

What's gone wrong?

After such a cheering start, the brothers must have looked forward to their next "flying season" with high hopes. When they went back to Kitty Hawk in July 1901, they were full of confidence. They had built a bigger, more powerful machine. They had the support and advice of Chanute, by now very interested in their project. They even had the company of two of Chanute's protégés, one with medical training.

In their new camp, close to the Kill Devil Hills themselves, the Wrights were all set to have a splendid time.

In fact, they had a worrying one.

Things went wrong from the start. It rained; then the brothers were ill. With the dry weather came clouds of bloodthirsty mosquitoes, that plagued the camp day and night. One of Chanute's friends turned out to be a fool and a bore. And – worst of all – the new machine did not fly as well as the old one.

At a moment's notice, it would go out of control. Once, with Wilbur aboard, it rose to forty feet and almost stopped moving: just the same situation that led to Lilienthal's death. Happily, it recovered from this near-stall, and delivered the startled Wilbur to earth again.

One problem was the new camber the brothers had built into the wings. It was the one Lilienthal had used. But it seemed too sharp, too extreme.

Wilbur and Orville went back to their original camber – and then found other doubts crowding in on them. There was so much else they still didn't understand.

In August, the Wrights came home unexpectedly, oddly silent about flying. Wilbur went straight to bed with a cold, almost too depressed to speak. Why go on? It was obvious they didn't know what they were doing. No one did. The experts were mistaken, the books wrong or silent. At this rate, it would be fifty years before anyone achieved true mechanical flight.

Wilbur was about to give up.

Chanute to the rescue

It was Chanute who came to the rescue. He knew, none better, that the brothers had already broken all gliding records ever made. He'd seen them in action, too, having stayed a week at the Kill Devil camp. They now knew more about flying than anyone else alive – or dead. They had to go on.

Before the month was up, he had cured Wilbur's despair by – very shrewdly – giving him something else to worry about. The elder Wright was invited to give a talk to a grand professional body, the Western Society of Civil Engineers. The subject, of course, was the work at Kitty Hawk.

Wilbur came out of his depression in a trice. Reserved and modest, he at first wanted to refuse the invitation. But his sister bullied him into accepting. Rigged up in the dapper Orville's best clothes, Wilbur overcame his stage-fright and gave a magnificent lecture.

He did more. He publicly questioned the value of the figures that had been published so far on mechanical flight.

At home in Dayton, it was Orville's turn to feel nervous. The figures that Wilbur was challenging had been produced by some of the best scientific brains of the time. But the Wrights weren't scientists; they hadn't even been to college. They'd got into flying purely for fun. So what did Will think he was doing?

Wing Sections of Stuffed Birds

The key to flight: what a bird's wing looks like when seen *from the side*. It is the way *air behaves* when flowing over a shape like this that takes a man-made "bird" off the ground. The specimens shown here were drawn by the Wrights' friend and expert adviser, Octave Chanute. The curve that the brothers built into the wings of their aircraft was halfway between the buzzard shape and the herring gull one.

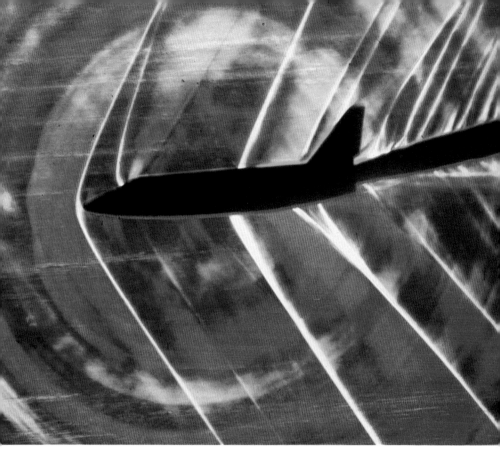

From the Wrights' time, tests have played a vital part in designing aircraft. The bottom photograph opposite shows the Wrights' own testing station: the workroom behind the cycle shop, where the home-made wind tunnel stood. The inside of a wind-tunnel of the 1970s is shown opposite above, during tests on a space shuttle design. The picture above shows a different test method, computer simulation. Computer graphics are being used to show the movement of air over a F-16 jet.

Uncharted territory

There was only one way for Orville to ease his anxiety. He had to re-check those figures for himself. Kitty Hawk was now far away, but that was no problem. He rigged up a miniature wind-tunnel in an old box, and spent several hours testing models of curved wing-surfaces. By the end of the day, he had an answer. The published figures *were* wrong. The question now was: how much?

When Wilbur came back, this new riddle proved just what he needed to prevent his blues returning. He and Orville plunged into a large-scale testing project. They built a bigger wind-tunnel and, in an air-current produced by a gas-driven fan, they tested over two hundred different sorts of wing surface: long ones and short ones; thick ones and thin ones; singles, doubles, even triples, stacked one on top of each other.

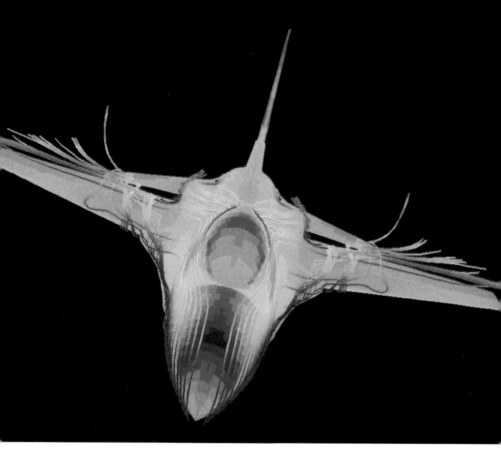

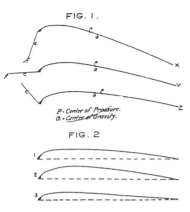

FIG. 1.

P.·Center of Pressure.
G.·Center of Gravity.

FIG. 2

Wilbur used these diagrams in his Chicago lecture to show what happened when an aerofoil – the top wing of their glider – was flown as a kite in different strengths of wind. A light wind made it fly up at the end of its cord (top drawing); a very strong one pulled it down. Compare the wing's shape with the sections through the birds' wings shown on page 37.

Which had the best lift? Which suffered most from friction with the air? What happened when the angle of attack – the "angle of incidence" – was changed? How did everything behave? Carefully, Wilbur noted the results and sent their findings off to Chanute: column after column of figures, marching down the pages in Will's neat writing.

The Wrights were now entering areas of knowledge where no one – however famous or highly-qualified – had ever been before. The brothers ranged over this uncharted territory for only two months; by Christmas, it was again time to prepare for the spring bicycle rush. But, by then, they had identified and recorded the conditions that will allow a heavier-than-air machine to fly.

Without meaning to, they had joined the foremost ranks of the world's scientific pioneers.

The new camp

It went without saying that they'd go back to Kitty Hawk. Thanks to their own figures, they now knew what they were meant to be doing. All they wanted now was to try doing it. By August 1902, they were fretting around the house in Hawthorn Street, sewing wing-covers for a new glider and growing more nervy by the day. "They will be all right when they get down in the sand," commented Katharine wisely.

There was another delay when, at the end of the month, they got back to their old camp by the Kill Devil Hills. The sands and winds of Kitty Hawk had half-buried the shed in which they now kept their machine, and they had to repair it. They also added on living space for themselves. But, in September, their flying season could start in earnest.

In their new machine, they went up over a thousand times. They took off into gale-force winds. They stayed airborne for forty seconds at a time; then fifty seconds, then a minute. This latest glider, based on their own research, had the lift of a bird and – almost all the time – the control of a drill-sergeant.

All it needed now was power.

Power for the machine

The next step was to get an engine: a petrol engine, naturally. The days when Wilbur could scoff at the future of the automobile were long gone. It was to the automobile companies that the brothers now turned. They wrote off letter after letter, asking firms if they would build a very special "one-off" – a powerful engine that weighed no more than 200lb. Everywhere, they met with disappointment.

So they built one themselves. Amazingly, they got it ready for testing in six weeks. And, when they ran it, they found they'd built a motor that was even lighter and stronger than the one they'd asked for.

The propeller gave them more trouble. They planned to copy the designs used for ships' propellers but, after more research in Dayton Public Library, they realized they would have to think again. The facts and figures they needed simply were not available. The ship builders of that time didn't design their propellers in advance. They just proceeded by trial and error, stopping when they had a propeller that worked.

Another long research period now faced the Wrights and, this time, even they felt daunted by the nightmarish problems involved. A propeller, they reasoned, behaved like an aerofoil moving in a spiral course. But how could that movement be observed and tested? As Orville commented later: "It is hard to find even a point from which to make a start; for nothing about a propeller, or the medium in which it acts, stands still for a moment."

"The thrust," he went on, "depends upon the speed and the angle at which the blade strikes the air; the angle at which the blade strikes the air depends upon the speed at which the propeller is turning, the speed the machine is traveling forward, and the speed at which the air is slipping backward; the slip of the air backward depends upon the thrust exerted by the propeller, and the amount of air acted upon. When any one of these changes, it changes all the rest."

In the end, incredibly, the brothers managed to

> *"The genius that begins at the beginning and builds up by conscientious study of elementary points – which many hastily assume they understand – is well exemplified in his character. In addition, he and his brother possessed a remarkable aptitude for supplementing each other's efforts, and it was that unity of purpose and perfect understanding which brought them success."*
>
> M.J.B. Davy.

> *"Those who formerly had lifted themselves from the surface of the earth had been too dependent upon the natural forces that they had utilized…. The Wrights showed how it was possible to fly into the wind."*
>
> Michael Harrison, from "Airborne at Kitty Hawk".

To soar like a bird: the dream that, for centuries, had inspired so many inventors, and consumed so much of their thought and time. For some, it was a dream that led to their deaths – a risk that always hung over the Wrights as they brought their own dream closer and closer to reality.

solve this as well. And, when they returned to their practice-ground in September 1903, they were again full of confidence.

The first launch

There were, of course, the usual delays. As before, they found that the Kill Devil camp was the worse for wear. So they did repairs to the old shed, and built a second one beside it. After that, the weather turned stormy, hurling down winds that – at 75 mph – bordered on hurricane strength. Then it rained; later it snowed.

There were problems with the machine, too. When the motor was tried out on the ground, things broke or worked loose. Usually, the broken parts had to go back to Dayton for replacement, but the brothers carried out one on-the-spot repair themselves. They fixed the loose parts together with the rubber cement they used in making bicycle wheels.

At last, by December 14, everything was ready: the aircraft, the launching equipment, and the launch assistants. These were the men of the nearby Kill Devil Life Saving station, who were fascinated by the experiments further up their lonely beach. In the calm of a fine winter's afternoon, they helped the Wrights haul the machine up Big Kill Devil Hill, and adjust its launching-rail.

Wilbur and Orville tossed a coin to decide who would try out the machine first, and Wilbur won. He slid into the pilot's place on the lower wing, while Orville steadied it at one end. The engine throbbed; the wire holding the machine in place was released. Then everything began to happen very quickly.

The machine, rushing forward, tore itself from Orville's grasp in an instant. An instant more, and it was lifting itself off the rail. It was climbing … it was climbing too far, and losing all its speed! It stalled.

Sagging back to the ground again, it caught a wing, spun round, and crunched to a halt. The trial was over.

Wilbur had been airborne for just three and a half seconds.

The machine flies

It could have been worse, the brothers decided cheerfully as they checked the plane over. It was not badly damaged. The front rudder and one of the skids would need some repairs, but that was all. The Wrights now knew that their launching system worked. All in all, things were going well.

They spent the next day doing repairs, and part of the next. By afternoon on December 16, the machine was ready again. During the night, it got colder: when the brothers woke on Thursday, December 17, the puddles around the camp were covered with ice. And that wasn't the only change. The Kitty Hawk wind had got up, and was now blowing from the north at 27mph.

The moment when the world changed. The date is December 17, 1903; the time is 10.35 in the morning. Orville has just taken off to make the world's first flight in a power-driven, heavier-than-air machine. Wilbur, who steadied the plane while it moved down the launching rail from the left, is still half-running: the prop that had held the wing up is in the middle of the picture. The photograph was taken on Orville's camera by Kill Devils lifeguard, John T. Daniels.

The brothers waited. And waited. Then they got tired of waiting.

They took their aircraft out on the sand-flats by the camp, and made it fly.

The moth out of season

With eyes narrowed against the wind, Orville watched as the little aircraft droned off on its fourth flight of the day. So did the other witnesses, whose names would later be famous: life-guards Daniels, W.S. Dough and A.D. Etheridge from Kill Devil; the elderly W.C. Brinkley, who'd retired to the area; and Johnny Moore, a local youth.

Flying over that sandy waste, the machine looked like some great pale moth – a moth out of season. It was utterly strange, utterly exotic. With its fragile wings, its twirling propellers and its thrumming engine, it belonged to a world that had not yet come. But, with every turn of the propellers, that world ventured closer and closer.

Orville's eyes narrowed further as, abruptly, the plane darted toward the ground. After a bumpy take-off, Will had been doing so well. But now the machine was pitching up and down, just as it had done on its first flight. It made one final swoop, hit the ground, and stayed motionless.

From where he stood, Orville tried to judge the distance. No doubt about it, this was the longest flight yet. Something like eight hundred feet; more, maybe. In their glider a year ago, they'd been happy to travel half that distance.

With a powered machine, who knew what they could do now?

Joyously, Orville and the rest hurried over the sands to where Wilbur and the machine waited for them. The plane showed signs of a rough landing: its front rudder was smashed. But what was that, compared to what it had achieved? The rudder could easily be repaired. The brothers and their helpers carried the machine back to the camp, and stood around talking.

"Inform press home Christmas"

Suddenly, as they talked, disaster struck. An extra-strong gust of wind came tearing along the sand, caught the aircraft, and flipped it over. Grabbing where they could, everyone dived to the rescue. But the machine rolled over and over, taking John Daniels with it. When finally helped to his feet, he was bruised and shaken. But the aircraft had come off much worse. The wings were buckled, their wooden ribs smashed, the engine damaged. There would be no more flying that year.

But there would always be next year ... and the next. And all the years to come. To be getting on with, four powered flights were enough.

Vanishing into their shed, Wilbur and Orville Wright made lunch, ate it, washed the dishes, and then set off to Kitty Hawk to send a telegram back to Dayton. "Success four flights Thursday morning," it read. "Inform press home Christmas."

The story that went begging

In Dayton, the Wright family did as the brothers asked. They informed the press, who were not particularly interested. Meanwhile on the coast, an

"With all the knowledge and skill acquired in thousands of flights in the last ten years, I would hardly think today of making my first flight on a strange machine in a twenty-seven-mile wind, even if I knew that the machine had already been flown and was safe. After these years of experience I look with amazement upon our audacity in attempting flights with a new and untried machine under such circumstances."
Orville Wright, describing the first powered flight at Kitty Hawk on December 17, 1903.

enterprising young journalist heard of the Wrights' achievement from a telegraph operator. He, too, tried to sell the story to the newspapers but, for the most part, they weren't interested either. Only three papers printed the story the next morning – and they did not include Dayton's own *Journal!*

The scoop of the world was going begging that December, and few people realized it. Astonishingly, it would be five years before the fame the brothers deserved caught up with them.

This is really the oddest part of the whole Wright story. Between 1903 and 1908, the Wrights went on with their great project in the full view of anyone who cared to look. And everyone, it seemed, persisted in looking the other way.

Two forces were at work in keeping this communications gap so big. For a start, the journalists, government officials, and millions of ordinary people who had not seen the Wrights fly simply did not believe that they had.

The world, they all agreed, was full of cranks, claiming they could fly like angels – and, so far, these claims had always been false. Powered flight was one of the ultimate challenges facing the scientist, and everyone knew that progress was slow. Why, that very year, even Professor Samuel Langley had twice failed to make his new machine fly. Obviously, these bicycle-makers from Ohio were just two more deluded crackpots.

Not in their own backyard

The people who *had* seen the Wrights fly were in a different position. They knew they could believe the evidence of their eyes. What they did not believe was the importance of that evidence.

Most of them were ordinary working people: life-guards, farmers, traders, and members of Dayton's business community. Most of them had little to do with the wider world of the news media, let alone that of aviation. They vaguely knew that people were trying to fly. They'd also heard that a rich Brazilian named Alberto Santos-Dumont was doing amazing things in Paris: flying round the Eiffel Tower.

Of course, they also knew the Wrights were flying around all over a weed-grown field near Dayton. But they did not realize that there was a difference between the exotic Brazilian and their own home-grown aviators. Santos-Dumont was flying the very latest lighter-than-air machine: a balloon with an engine attached. The Wrights' aircraft was the very first successful, full-scale, powered, heavier-than-air craft; the world's first aeroplane.

People seldom think that history is made in their own backyard. The people of Dayton were no exception.

Above: The early work of the Wright brothers was often dismissed as madness – but it was the beginning of a new era. This passenger-carrying aircraft is a common sight today but was only a fantastic dream in 1903.

"At it again"

In one way, this lack of publicity was a blessing for Wilbur and Orville. It meant they could get on with their flying without interruptions. In 1904, they built a new, stronger aircraft – "Flyer II", as they called it – to replace the mangled but triumphant "Flyer I" of Kitty Hawk. Then they set up a new practice-ground: a cow pasture eight miles outside Dayton, called the Huffman Prairie after its owner.

Here, during the next two years, they brought the art of flying to an astonishing level of expertise.

Two roads and a railway ran by the Prairie, so the brothers were never short of passers-by to witness their aerobatics. There was often plenty to see. The flights were getting longer so, to stay within the limits of the field, the Wrights taught themselves to turn in the air. They started to circle the field: once, twice, several times.

By late summer 1905, their flight mileages were entering double figures. In September, the "grandson" of "Flyer I" – "Flyer III" – achieved an uninterrupted flight of twelve miles. Within a few days, this record looked puny beside the new one "Flyer III" had set – twenty-four miles, flown in thirty-eight minutes.

The local onlookers took these achievements calmly. Calmest of all was the next-door farmer, Amos Stauffer. For Stauffer, the Wrights were just part of the landscape. "Well, the boys are at it again," he'd say, when he saw the "Flyer" in action. Interviewed by a visitor in 1905, he recalled that he "just kept on stooking corn until I got down to the fence, and the durned thing was still going round. I thought it would never stop."

Is the Army interested?

In another way, the ignorance that veiled the Wrights' exploits was not a blessing, but a curse. The brothers had their living to earn. At first, they did not expect to earn it from the hobby that had become an obsession. But, after 1903, things began to look different. Wilbur and Orville now knew they had invented something of value: something that might be useful to businesses – or to governments.

Naturally, they wanted to give their own government the first option on any deal. They had, they told their member of Congress, invented a machine that could be used in war, for "scouting and carrying messages". Would the Army be interested?

For a long while, the United States' Army reacted

Wilbur was famous for the total attention he paid to any technical problem, however small. Here, he concentrates on a kite belonging to the son of pilot Frank Coffyn (left). Coffyn was one of the earliest pilots to graduate from the training school the Wrights set up in Dayton.

just like the United States' press. They didn't believe a word of it. In Europe, however, the top brass was less short-sighted. The British started making inquiries about what the Wrights had to sell. So did the French.

In France and Germany, questions had also begun to be asked in aviation circles. Slowly, the publicity that the Americans had denied the Dayton brothers was building up abroad.

Wheelings and dealings

The French aviators got so interested that they sent someone on a fact-finding mission to Dayton to see the Wrights for himself. This was the visitor who, in 1905, talked to farmer Stauffer. "Claims completely verified," was the message he sent back to France at the end of his trip.

Soon, the Wrights were deep in negotiations with the French and, in 1906, the European connection became even more active. That year and the next, the brothers visited France, then Germany. The air-minded Germans were already developing their great Zeppelin airships; now they were interested in aircraft as well!

Meanwhile, the United States' Army was at last beginning to shed its massive disinterest. Just before Christmas in 1907, in an invitation clearly aimed at the Wrights, it asked anyone who could supply flying machines to state his terms.

In the early months of 1908, the brothers' lives speeded up still further. Deals were now close with both the United States' Government and a group of top-level French businessmen. But, before everything was settled, both wanted to see the new invention in action. So, in May, Wilbur set off for France, while Orville remained at home to do the official United States' trials at Fort Myer.

Of the two, it was the shy, introspective Wilbur who would have the more dazzling time. His French visit turned into a triumphal progress through Europe, which lasted into 1909. When Orville later joined him, it would be after a very different set of adventures.

Orville (left) watches a flight at Le Mans with English balloonist Griffith Brewer. While visiting the Wrights in France, Brewer became the first Englishman ever to fly in an aeroplane.

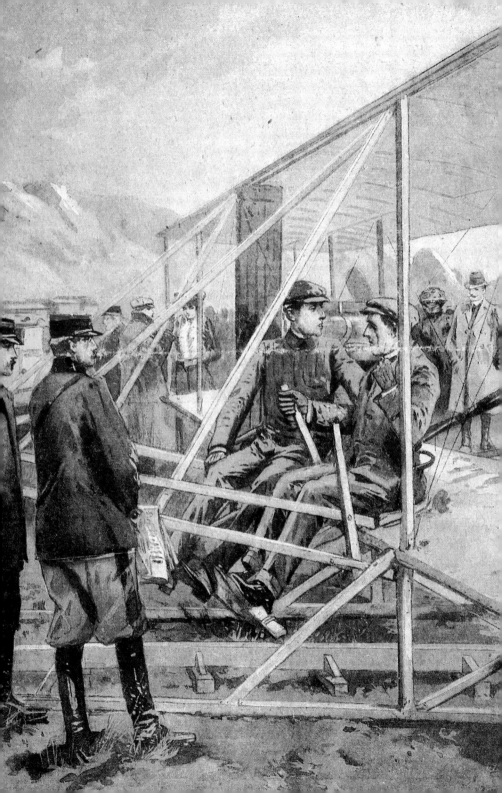

Wilbur conquers France

Wilbur's tour started in Le Mans where, on August 8, he began his trial flights on a local racecourse. The crowds who turned out to see him went wild with enthusiasm. The thin American really could do what he promised: he had indeed conquered the air! Within a few days, he had conquered the French. Unassuming, patient and good-natured, he won over everyone who met him.

The workers in the factory where he assembled his aircraft were deeply touched by his democratic style: he worked the same hours as them, and ate in the same place. Meanwhile, businessmen, journalists and aviators vied with each other in their admiration. Women were completely bowled over by the dashing aviator with the lean face and the broad smile. Fanmail poured in by the sackful.

Wilbur bore it all well. In September, he even unbent enough to admit that Madame Berg, wife of one of his French hosts, was a "jolly woman and very intelligent". She would later become the first woman ever to go up in an aeroplane. But then, only a few days later, news reached him from the United States that put paid to cheerfulness.

The Army trials at Fort Myer had been suspended. Orville's machine had crashed; Orville himself was seriously injured. And an army officer who'd gone up with him had been killed.

First blood

Back in the States, Orville's summer had been going well too. When, in August, he arrived at Fort Myer for the trials, he was dismayed to find that the flying area was very small. However, he turned a problem into an advantage, and astounded the crowds with the performances he extracted from his aircraft.

The records set on the Huffman Prairie now dwindled into nothingness; Orville was quickly notching up flights of over an hour, and rising to heights of two hundred feet and more. The Army deal looked more and more of a certainty.

And then, on September 17, 1908, the unthinkable happened.

Opposite: Although protocol kept the King of Spain firmly grounded during his visit to Pau, Wilbur was still able to teach him how the "Flyer's" controls worked. By this time, the Wrights and their passengers flew sitting up. But, once they were airborne, there was still very little to keep them in the 'plane. Below: the accident at Fort Myer, reconstructed by a French artist. The caption reads: "The bird-men: the aviators' terrible crash."

Le Petit Parisien
Supplément Littéraire Illustré

LES HOMMES-VOLANTS
TERRIBLE CHUTE D'AVIATEURS

By this time, the pilot of a Wright plane flew in a sitting position, and there was space for a passenger alongside. Orville had already taken two passengers aloft. Now a third wanted a go: Lieutenant Thomas Selfridge, aged twenty-six. For the first few minutes of the flight, all went well. Then Orville began to sense something was wrong with the machine. He was about to start a hurried descent when, abruptly, it veered out of control.

Desperately, Orville fought to bring the machine down safely. And he all but succeeded; he was, after all, one of the two most experienced flyers in the world. But gravity, in the end, was stronger.

The plane crashed headlong into the ground. Selfridge, whose skull was fractured, died later that day in hospital. By some miracle, Orville escaped with no more than a broken leg, broken ribs, and – an injury that went undiagnosed for twelve years – three hip fractures.

The crash was the first fatal accident in modern aviation history. The new invention had drawn its first blood. And, in doing so, it announced to the world in banner headlines that the age of air travel had dawned.

Horrified to hear of Selfridge's death, Wilbur cancelled the trials for a few days. He felt personally responsible for the tragedy. If he'd been at Fort Myer, he kept thinking, it would not have happened. He could have taken some of the weight off Orville's shoulders; helped with the preparation, the checking, or the time-consuming chats with visitors. But the inner toughness that, long ago, had pulled him out of illness and depression again came to his rescue. He accepted the guilt – and got on with the job.

Glory days

In his hospital bed in the United States, Orville was being just as tough-minded. Someone asked if he'd lost his nerve. Far from it, he replied: the only thing that worried him was getting well in time to finish the Army tests the following year.

In November, he came out of hospital. In early

1909, he had joined Wilbur in France, taking with him the staunch Katharine. With the winter, flying operations had been moved to Pau, in south-western France. And it was here that the Wrights entered their glory days.

By now, a French company had been set up to deal in Wright planes. Wilbur's main job now was training its pilots. Although Orville and Katharine were put up at Pau's best hotel, he went on sleeping in the hangar beside his plane, just as he had at Le Mans. Quickly, it became the most-visited shed in France – and the visitors got grander by the day.

King Alfonso of Spain came to see the flying machine; so did King Edward VII of Britain. So did Lord Northcliffe, owner of the British newspaper, the *Daily Mail*, who later that year would stage a competition for pilots to fly the English Channel. The race was won by the French aviator Louis Blériot, in his own monoplane "Blériot XI". By now, encouraged by what they'd heard of the Wrights' work in the United States, the French were also developing aircraft of their own.

King Alfonso longed to go up in Wilbur's machine. But he was prevented by his wife and his government ministers. However, no such restrictions weighed on Katharine Wright, who went up twice.

From Pau, the Wrights went on to Italy, where they flew before King Victor Emmanuel. Here again, deals to sell the Wright plane got under way, and Wilbur started training Italian flyers. While he was at it, he was approached again by the Germans, whose interest had been growing steadily. Now they wanted to set up a Wright plane company too....

Dayton welcomes its own

And so the glory days went on. Crowned heads, business deals, presentations, medals: these had now become everyday features of the Wrights' lives. In May 1909, they went back to the States, where their home town was waiting for them. The people of Dayton, making up for their earlier lack of excitement, staged an official "welcome" that lasted two days.

Flying gear: Wilbur, here seen piloting his sister Katharine, wears his usual flat cap and leather jacket. Katharine has tied a string around her skirts to stop them flapping. Visible in the background are one of the "Flyer's" propellers and the uprights of its back rudder, or tail. The Wrights began to add tails to their aircraft in 1902.

In many countries – although not in the USA – governments quickly realized that the newly-invented aeroplane could be used as a weapon. As shown above (top) and opposite, the first World War of 1914-1918 speeded up aircraft development dramatically. In both, the aeroplanes look much more like a modern aircraft than the Wrights' machines did. The third picture shows war aircraft being used over Mexico.

Their real-life welcome was spectacular enough: the brothers and Katharine left the station in a lantern-lit carriage procession, and *ten thousand* people thronged to meet them at Hawthorn Street. But this was nothing compared to the celebrations the following month. These started at nine in the morning on June 17, when all the bells and factory whistles in Dayton sounded at once. Flags flew, bands played, and Wilbur and Orville rode in procession through the wildly cheering crowds. In the evening, there were fireworks; the next day, there were two more parades, and the brothers received medals from Congress, from the state of Ohio, and from their own home city.

54

What happened to the joy?

For the Wrights themselves, Dayton's celebration was only one fixture among many on a hectic schedule. Hardly had the cheers died down when the Wrights were back in Washington, completing their interrupted trials at Fort Myer. No sooner had the Army deal been triumphantly completed when Orville and Katharine were off to Europe again. They were bound for Berlin, where Orville would start a training course for German fliers of the Wright machine. Here, he met the famous Count von Zeppelin himself and – of course – the German royal family. Meanwhile, in New York, Wilbur

"Orville has a way of stepping right into the affections of nice people whom he meets, and they will be nice to you at first for him and then for yourself, for you have some little knack in that line yourself."

Wilbur Wright, in a letter to Katharine Wright, 1908.

55

Orville in later life, now dressed in the classic aviator's garb of leathers and close-fitting helmet. Technology never lost its fascination for him. The last problem he tried to solve – only hours before the heart attack that killed him – was mending a fault in the bell-pull system at Hawthorn Hill.

raised American air-mindedness another notch by flying twenty-one miles along the Hudson River.

Orville and Katharine returned at the start of November; by the end of it, the United States had its own Wright Company, and this made the brothers' diary even more crowded still. There were pilots to train, a factory to build and run (in Dayton, of course), aircraft to test, and flying exhibitions to give to stir public interest up still further.

It was very hard work. And, sadly, the Wrights found they were being taken further and further from what they really wanted to do. As they'd learned in the exhilarating days of Kitty Hawk, flying was their joy; research their special delight. And now they'd become wealthy businessmen, striking deals and fighting designers who infringed their patents. For company president Wilbur, who dealt with these legal worries, chances to fly started to become thin on the ground.

In May 1910, the Wright president went up by himself for a short spin over Huffman Prairie. He little knew that it would be the last he would ever make as a pilot. Twenty-four months later, on May 30, 1912, he died from typhoid fever. He was just forty-five years old.

Orville alone

For Orville, the surviving partner, life carried on. He took Wilbur's place as president of the company, and attended to its business. In 1915, he sold all his interest in it. Then he went back to the research that he and Wilbur had loved so much. He mixed in the topmost circles in both industry and flying, and met people like the car manufacturer Henry Ford and the pilot Charles Lindbergh, who in 1927 flew solo from New York to Paris.

Orville must have been lonely without his brother, but he never tried to make up for his loss by marrying. Perhaps he did not feel the need to. After all, the family ties that had sustained the great partnership were still intact. He still had his two other brothers and their children; he still had his devoted sister, Katharine, and his father, now eighty-four but as kindly and keen-minded as ever.

Indeed Bishop Wright had now become a flyer like the rest of them. Just after Wilbur made his last solo flight, his brother had taken their father up for his very first experience of the air. They reached three hundred and fifty feet; "higher, higher," the intrepid old man said.

Two years after Wilbur's death, Orville moved with his father and sister into a large new house outside Dayton, called Hawthorn Hill. Setting it up was the last project that he and Will had worked on together. The Bishop died in 1917, and Katharine married and moved away in the 1920s. But Orville stayed there for the rest of his life, watching as the gift he and Wilbur had given the world changed that same world out of all recognition.

The legacy

Even before Wilbur's death, the changes had begun to mount up. In 1909, Blériot flew the English Channel in his monoplane, easily overtaking the steamship sent to escort him, and then losing it completely. In 1910, a British pilot hit on the novel idea of carrying letters by air.

The same year, an Ohio department store hired a Wright plane to make the world's first-ever express delivery by air: a roll of silk, carried at a speed of over a mile a minute. Only the very fastest cars could do better – and they had to go where roads took them. And an express train like the famous Twentieth Century Limited, running between New York and Chicago, was slower. It took about twenty hours to cover its thousand miles of iron tracks.

Already, a few people's ideas of time and distance were beginning to change. The world was starting to shrink. By the time Wilbur died in 1912, it was shrinking further and faster.

Unlike the Americans, the governments of Europe had been quick to spot the military potential of the flying machines. When World War I broke out in 1914, aircraft were already being built that could fly at 90 mph. By the end of it, Europe's airspace was ruled by fighter planes like the German Fokkers and the British Sopwith Camel, with its

Societa Italiana **DUNLOP**
MILANO ROMA

A high-fashion occasion for rich Italians: an air show held in 1928. As in Wilbur Wright's time, shows like this went on playing an important part in promoting interest in flying. By now, wealthy people like the ones shown here could experience flying for themselves, in aircraft built for passenger travel.

"They had not only made the first wind-tunnel in which miniature wings were accurately tested, but were the first men in all the world to compile tables of figures from which one might design an aeroplane that could fly. Even today ... the refinements obtained over the Wrights' figures for the same shapes of surfaces are surprisingly small."

*Fred C. Kelly,
from his biography,
"The Wright Brothers".*

The story of flight continues, both inside and outside the earth's atmosphere. *Above:* with the narrow "delta" shape of its backswept wings outlined by scaffolding, the supersonic airliner Concorde undergoes maintenance. The space shuttle shown below has the same swept-back outline.

top speed of 113mph. Meanwhile, the heavier machines used for bombing had begun to fly distances of hundreds of miles.

It was in a converted bomber that, in 1919, the British-based aviators John Alcock and Arthur Whitten Brown made the world's first flight across the Atlantic: a distance of almost 1,900 miles. It took them three minutes short of sixteen hours. A hundred years earlier, when people crossed the Atlantic in sailing ships, it had taken twenty-three days. It would still be taking four days in the fastest luxury liners of the 1930s.

After the war, people realized that the long-range aircraft could make money. The old bombers were

Dusseldorf Airport, [West] Germany: tended by airport staff, the world-shrinkers of today gleam sleekly in the sun. The scene seems a whole world away from Kitty Hawk and the Kill Devil Hills. But the principles underlying modern aricraft design remain the same as the ones that obsessed the Wrights almost a hundred years ago, and that were triumphantly conquered on a wind-combed beach in 1903.

59

quickly converted into passenger aircraft and, in the 1920s and 1930s, a whole new transport system was offered to those who could afford it. Organized air travel had added itself to the far older (and slower) options of travel by land and sea.

World War II, when it started in 1939, again gave extra impetus on the development of flight. One by one, inventions that had been born in peacetime received their first full use in war: radar, the jet engine, the helicopter. And again, when peace came back, all three would go on transforming the world their users lived in.

Orville's death

Orville Wright died, aged seventy-six, on January 30, 1948, three years after aircraft had been used to drop the deadliest weapon of war ever invented: the atomic bomb.

He had already lived to see politicians hurrying around the world in his invention, making decisions that would affect millions. He had seen it used for advertising, trailing messages to boost a business's sales. In Europe, it carried the wealthy from one tourist spot to another; in Australia, it brought medical aid to isolated sheep stations. But these pre-war uses were small-scale compared to what would come later, as machines got bigger and air transport became commonplace.

Thanks to the Wrights' legacy, we now live in a world where we can eat strawberries in winter. If we jet off to Chile, we can also go skiing in June. If illness threatens the life of someone in France, a rare drug can be flown in from Japan to help. If there is a family wedding on the other side of the world, a mother can be there. When disaster strikes a country anywhere on earth, planes can bring in food, medicines and rescue workers.

When Wilbur and Orville Wright launched their "Flyer I" at Kitty Hawk in 1903, the peoples of the world were kept apart as much by distance and time as by their warring beliefs. Today, both distance and time have lost their power to divide – and rule.

"Achievement followed achievement in the air with such bewildering rapidity that, by the year 1948 when Orville Wright died, the world could no longer marvel. But then, what flight that ever followed – no, not even man's rocketing into space – could match the wonderful achievement and sheer courage of those first breathless twelve seconds in the air that memorable day in December, 1903, or equal it in significance as the herald of a new age?"

John Canning, from "100 Great Lives".

Scientific Terms

Aerofoil (also "airfoil"): The shape in which an aircraft wing is built. When seen in cross-section, this shape is curved above and flat below. At the front of the wing, the curve dips sharply down to a rounded edge. Without this curved upper surface, *Bernoulli's Principle* could not operate.

Angle of attack: The angle – a gentle upward slope – at which an aircraft wing meets the air flowing over and under it. In the Wrights' time, this was called the "angle of incidence".

Bernoulli's Principle: A physical law stating that, if a moving fluid or gas moves faster, the pressure it exerts decreases. It is named after the Swiss mathematician Daniel Bernoulli who, in the eighteenth century, studied the movement of fluids. It is the basic law underpinning the science of aerodynamics, or the way moving gases and objects behave when they interact. See also *lift*, below.

Camber: The hump-backed curve made by the top of an *aerofoil*; the curve can be of many different shapes, from steep to shallow.

"Chinese flying top": A spinning-top equipped with an airscrew or *propeller;* when spun quickly, the *propeller* carried the top into the air, just as the rotors do on a modern helicopter. Flying tops are a very ancient form of toy.

Drag: Friction between the air and a moving aircraft wing, acting to hold the aircraft back. One of the four forces always in action on a moving heavier-than-air machine; the others are *lift*, gravity, and the forward thrust exerted by whatever form of power the machine uses.

Elevator: A moveable part of an aircraft that controls upward and downward movement. On the Wrights' gliders and aeroplanes, the elevators were at the front of the machine. On modern aircraft, they form part of the tail at the back.

Flaps: Moveable sections of a modern aeroplane wing, giving control over *lift* and *drag*. They have replaced the *wing-warping* system used by the Wright brothers, but have the same effect.

Free flight: A powered heavier-than-air machine is in free flight when it can be kept by its own power on a level or upward course, and continue further on this course than the distance that it could glide if unpowered. An important definition of what the Wrights were trying to achieve.

Gale force: On the Beaufort Scale used for measuring wind, the "gale" entries are among the more violent winds. They range from moderate gale (32-38 mph) to whole gale (55-63 mph).

Glider: A heavier-than-air flying machine without a built-in power supply. After take-off (either artificially-powered or from a height), gliders slowly fly forward and downward, pulled by gravity.

Heavier-than-air flight: Flight in aircraft such as aeroplanes, gliders, or helicopters. Some heavier-than-air machines, such as gliders, do not carry their own power supply. But, in order to fly, all need a power source, such as gravity or the petrol engine. Light steam engines have also been used.

Incidence, angle of: See *angle of attack*.

Lift: The force that lifts or "sucks" an aircraft wing upward, originating in the unequal pressures exerted by the air moving over and under the wing. See *Bernoulli's Principle*.

Lighter-than-air flight: Flight in hot-air balloons or balloons filled with some other gas, such as helium. The earliest lighter-than-air machines drifted before the wind. Then inventors tried attaching engines to them but, although these could drive the balloon along in calm weather, they were inefficient in wind. Later on, when the petrol engine was developed, lighter-than-air flight became much more effective, and culminated in the formidable *Zeppelins* developed in Germany.

"Montgolfière": A hot-air balloon, as developed by the Montgolfier brothers of France in the eighteenth century.

Propeller: A circular arrangement of *aerofoils*, fixed to a central rod. As the rod is turned, the propeller blades are sucked forward. (See *lift*.)

Skids: The runners of the sledge-like undercarriage of the Wrights' "Flyer".

Smithsonian Institution: A famous body in the USA that was set up in Washington in 1864 to promote learning and increase its spread.

Stall: For an aircraft to fly, it has to be moving fast enough through the air. If it slows down too much, it will stop flying, or stall.

Wing-warping: The system invented by the Wrights to control the *lift* of their aircraft wings, by changing the shape each presented to the air. On a modern aircraft, flaps do the same job.

Zeppelin: A huge, sausage-shaped, lighter-than-air flying machine, or airship, developed at the start of the twentieth century and named after its inventor, Count Ferdinand von Zeppelin.

Important Dates

1783 Nov 21: The world's first manned flight is staged in a hot-air balloon, developed by the Montgolfier brothers of Annonay, France.

1804 The British inventor, Sir George Cayley, builds his first glider, the world's first practical heavier-than-air flying machine.

1842 In Britain, William Samuel Henson patents a design for an aeroplane, his "Aerial Steam Carriage".

1848 In Britain, John Stringfellow's model aeroplane is successfully flown, indoors and out.

1867 April 16: Wilbur Wright is born near Millville, Indiana.

1871 Aug 19: Orville Wright is born in Dayton, Ohio.

1892 Wilbur and Orville set up their Wright Cycle Company in Dayton, Ohio.

1896 The German aviation pioneer, Otto Lilienthal, dies in a glider crash.

1899 May: Wilbur writes to the Smithsonian Institution for help with information on flying.
July-Aug: The Wrights make successful experiments with "wing-warping" and a kite.

1900 The Wrights' first glider trials are held at Kitty Hawk, North Carolina.

1901 July-Aug: The Wrights' second glider trials are held at the Kill Devil Hills, four miles south of Kitty Hawk. The Wrights are puzzled and discouraged by the mixed results achieved.
Sept: In Chicago, Wilbur addresses the Western Society of Civil Engineers. In Dayton, Orville starts wind-tunnel experiments.

1902 Successful trials of the glider based on the Wrights' wind-tunnel research are held at the Kill Devil Hills.

1903 Sept-Nov: At the Kill Devil Hills, the Wrights assemble their new, power-driven flying machine in readiness for their fourth set of flying trials.
Oct 17: Professor S.P. Langley tries out his full-sized, steam-powered aeroplane (called an "aerodrome") over the Potomac River; it fails to fly. A second trial in December also ends in failure.
Dec 17: At the Kill Devil Hills south of Kitty Hawk, Wilbur and Orville Wright make the world's first powered, manned, self-launching, controlled and successfully sustained flights in a heavier-than-air machine.

1904-5 With improved machines, the Wrights continue their flying trials at the Huffman Prairie, Dayton, Ohio.

1905-7 Interest in the Wrights' achievement grows, both in Europe and in the United States.

1908 Aug: Wilbur starts highly-successful flying demonstrations in France.
Sept 17: Orville is injured in flying trials staged for the US Army. His passenger, Thomas Selfridge, is killed: the first fatality in aeroplane flying.

1909 July: French aviator Louis Blériot flies the English Channel, taking forty-three minutes to cover thirty-one miles.
Nov: In the United States, the Wright Company is set up to build aeroplanes, and is instantly successful.

1912	May 30: Wilbur Wright dies, aged forty-five, after a sudden illness.
1914-18	World War I gives dramatic impetus to aircraft design and production.
1919	In an adapted Vickers-Vimy bomber, John Alcock and Arthur Whitten Brown become the first people to fly across the Atlantic. The flight of 1,890 miles takes fifteen hours, fifty-seven minutes.
1939	World War II breaks out. Once again, aircraft development is speeded up.
1945	World War II is brought to an end when atomic bombs are dropped in Hiroshima and Nagasaki in Japan.
1948	Jan 30: Orville Wright dies, aged seventy-six.

Further reading

A great deal has been written about Wilbur and Orville Wright, but much of it has appeared in magazines and essay collections, rather than in books. Much of it, too, is very technical. But there are two books you will enjoy reading if you want to find out more about the Wright brothers.

Fred C. Kelly: *The Wright Brothers*, Harrap, 1944. This is the official biography, checked over by Orville Wright himself; simple and easy to read.
Marvin W. McFarland (editor): *The Papers of Wilbur and Orville Wright*, McGraw-Hill, 1953. Wilbur and Orville's letters, diaries, notes, and public speeches, with additions from Katharine and Bishop Wright. Start by reading Katharine's letters. Then move on to Orville's, which are often very funny. Wilbur's are frequently technical, but his lecture to the Western Engineers is one of the simplest (and best) pieces of writing in existence on flight and flying. Fascinating photographs, many by the Wrights themselves.

For younger readers

There are many books for younger readers on flying and transport in general. Three good ones are:

R. Kerrod, C. Pick and J.D. Storer: *Encyclopedia of Transport*, Hamlyn, 1983.
Peter Lane: *Flight*, Batsford, 1974.
Susan Ward (editor): *The World of Transport*, Macdonald Educational, 1976.

Also recommended:
David Macaulay with Neil Ardley: *The Way Things Work*, Dorling Kindersley, 1988. A brilliantly illustrated (and often hilarious) guide to technology. An ideal starting-point for any technical reading.

Index